all the live-long day

poems by

JV BRUMMELS

*Hanna —
great tw—
in Omaha
JVBrum*

STEPHEN F. AUSTIN STATE UNIVERSITY PRESS

For more information:
Stephen F. Austin State University Press
P.O. Box 13007 SFA Station
Nacogdoches, Texas 75962
sfapress@sfasu.edu
www.sfasu.edu/sfapress

Publishing Manager: Kimberly Verhines
Book design: Jerri Bourrous
Distributed by Texas A&M Consortium
www.tamupress.com

ISBN: 978-1-62288-910-5

CONTENTS

Rise Up So Early in the Morning 2016

    Ghost Country . . . 7

    Punchline . . . 9

    Spring Break . . . 10

    Fools . . . 11

    Derby Day . . . 14

    Right Side of History . . . 16

    The Poor Mouth Talking Cure . . . 18

    Sundown on the Grampas . . . 21

    Frontier Dead as Romance . . . 24

    Jump . . . 26

    A Long Way from the Heart . . . 27

    An Empty Country Owned by No One Here . . . 29

    Coda: Multiverse . . . 33

Dinah, Won't You Blow Your Horn

    Stations of the Cross . . . 37

    For the Duration . . . 39

    Bound Away . . . 43

    Los Caballos . . . 45

    White Buffalo . . . 48

    Kicking Up Iron . . . 49

    When All Blood Is Shadow . . . 51

    The Life . . . 53

    LA Suite . . . 54

Someone's in the Kitchen

    Howdy . . . 61

        Part of the art of road's knowing . . . 63

        It's all modern now . . . 66

        You see as a kid I composed a life . . . 70

        Verlene . . . 72

Verlene I will have another . . . 74

Winters now I drift . . . 77

Something's been off from the start . . . 78

Ma . . . 82

What's a cow know . . . 84

Must be hell . . . 87

Notes . . . 90

Acknowledgments . . . 91

Rise Up So Early in the Morn

Ghost Country

New Year's Day
that hermaphrodite of a semi-colon
in the middle of a sentence
            of months of long nights
my spirit an animal denned up
            against the cold
my body a drooping paunch
smoked and hanging by the hook
                of TV or bad book
a shamble from east window to west
            my usual calisthenic

A surprise then when I rise from dreams
            anchored by ordinary fears
to step out on my winter porch
in a town closed down
but for antiques and thrift stores
to meet a year that *feels* new

                    *

To celebrate
            neighbor Jack Rabbit
                    his pup and I count cows
between county road and willows
along the slack rope of creek below us

Thickets skylined along the rim
            of this cup of earth
hide caved-in barns and houses
            racoons have repurposed
among obsolete machinery –
rusting anachronisms the earth eats

Cornered in the wide open miles
        of emptying grid
in the hot box of a pickup cab
more than worry eats my insides out
more than leafless stands of trash trees
        scrub my history

                    *

The sun steps out from behind clouds
Each new winter day adds minutes
        of light
Cows graze into the north wind
this year's crop of fresh calves building
in warm bellies round as new worlds

And like Jack's piebald pup
bored with watching all this
        breathing room
each new year
        even the last
must sometime settle
        into the crook of my arm
and count on my ear to lick

Punchline

– Leap Year February

Poetry is failed standup
            – Jerry Seinfeld

I stride down these halls class days
among young studying postcard-sized screens
my bootheels clacking the hard certainty
some lazy faction of the crowd
longs for the granddaddy fascist in me

I keep a secret buzzing deep
in my simple-minded sense of justice
This time next year I won't be here
and when they ask *Who'll stand up*
I'll have already said *Not me*
except to gather in my change
            and leave a good tip

Theology's tired routine of other better lives
lost its actuarial charm an eternity past
All my relatives' genetics hiss
            Sky's the limit
while my habits predict I'm dead in ten
I've made a life flirting with regret
For all my bitching I'm the man
            I want to be

But for my species' arithmetic
any life's like some summer's housefly's
Even the jump of a short month's extra day
            doesn't sway my flight
My last hot breath will rise like my first cry
outside these ivy-crawling walls

[handwritten margin notes: "New Year, Leap Year... chronological?"; "real or his image?"; "why?"]

❋ 9 ❋

Spring Break
– March

Rub-a-dub-dub

I give the taxman short shrift
yawn wide into the dentist's masked face
get a smile perched like a kiss
       on the banker's countenance
shoot the shit with the doc
Still I'm slacking

Vacation means
I can't even play hooky
on an eighty-degree day
so I buy a horned Hereford bull
       I name Saint Paddy
a breed I override a partner
       to choose

I reside in the city on business
       and live in the green
just now poised at the roots
       of last year's grass
A simple choice –
       cows and horses
       golf and lawnmowers
I won't stand another clapboard day

Fools
        – April

Most of a foot of snow
heavy and wet as fresh concrete

I have a good talk with myself
take plenty of breathers
and promise me a cerveza
        or two
down the block at the Broken Antler
soon as my corner lot's shoveled

The last fronds of overcast in the linden's
        bare-knuckle branches
give over to blue
I meet my shadow on the snow

Crazy John coming back
        from the Baptist church
on his shoulders
        little spade
and worn-out witch broom
stops
        and shouts at my bent back

tells me of the latest son of a bitch
        to do him wrong
a State Patrol shadowing him
while he picked up cans
        along the highway
Told him he should chase them
        speedin sons-a-bitchin truckers
bout knocked me down

Called me homeless
Me
                dressed like this

                              *

By five the Antler's filled
            with blizzard trade
and in spite of the sun
            and our own survival
the froth on each draw's
            narrow and mean
curses drunk and drunk again
on property taxes
            eyeglasses and jobs
how hard the snow
            worked their machines
and *lazy Mexicans* —
Oh *some're good*

I read the muted TV news —
JC Penney's closing a hundred stores
including the first
            in Kimmerer Wyoming
where in the Sixties
            my friend saw boys
castrate lambs with their teeth

                              *

I'm standing on the corner
finding my sleeve in the wind
when my neighbor passes
            and I fall in with him

our mismatched cuffed denim legs
        in stride for a short block
hardly one language in common

My driveway
        my walks draw gray spaces
in twilit white that'll melt away
        in a day or two
I remind myself the beauty part's
        this American town's
not just whiney little bitches
        sucking oxygen
others can better use

I think *machine* and *horsepower*
        and *horse*
I smell *cow* on the breeze

Derby Day
– May

I'm a black cat in a back alley
            behind a bar
the afternoon before branding
racing home for an hour
            of fast-forwarded build up
to the greatest two minutes in sport

I'm a cowboy moseying
            off the curb
                        watching
cops at the cable company
            down the block
when some longshot Jesus
            corners a Pontiac Sunbird

To think I might have died

To think graduation's come
            and gone
teacher? my latest and last students
            scattered like shot

A year from now
            no grades to award
we'll brand in the first good weather
get a leg up on summer
and have nothing at all
            left to fret about
I'm a white beard
I'm two weak eyes

I'm a whiskerless schoolmarm
trying to be
a thirty-foot hard-twist snake
of an arena rope
tied hard and fast to the horn

when luck double-hocks a dogie
out of dust in air –
horse and calf and vaquero   *Spanish*
knotted

and no turning back
from my father's hands
that'll lace tomorrow's longer
softer line
across corral dirt
stack dallies around the horn
give and take all the way
to the branding fire

Sure
I miss a turn and lose a calf
again and now
but I've studied the lesson   *a teacher*
dark horses teach –   *studying?*
an education's learning
how much to let slip   *Life-long learner*
and when to let go

Right Side of History
– June

Sounds like an adventure
> – a young woman's response to my plans for tomorrow

I garden prairie flowers
in my big-brimmed bonnet
    to welcome bees
back to this savaged vestige
    of tall-grass prairie
a quarter-mile north
of a Cedar County correction line

Funny to return land
to something like a past
    I never lived
only sniffed back when I was a kid
on air ancient as bison
crossing a Holt County Kinkaid

I make supper of a plate of beans
and a cold cup of morning coffee
at my table indifferent ghosts
past wresting a living
    from wilderness
and the perfect freedom to starve

My relations gathered here
remind me of each time
    I've been both
dead certain and wrong
My clothes wear me out

I know nothing but this weather –
sundown a New Mexico sky
      all up the plains
a blue stripe of light
beneath some few far clouds
      masquerading
as purple mountain majesty

The Poor Mouth Talking Cure
– July

Weep all you little rains,
wail, wind, wail . . .
– "The Colorado Trail," anonymous

If I have a hometown it's these
houses peeling paint
      along wide leached streets
To stand for an old friend's funeral
is to know I'm the same asshole
      I was in high school

[handwritten: almost rhyme?]

The remains – big tanned forearms
crossed over the bib of fresh Key overalls
A rental casket returned before cremation
The same question in a long life's hangover –
what's this conversation I need to have

I stop along the way home to breathe
smoke into the blow of a big south wind
among trees I planted on land I used to own
a frontier bedeviling the particular
      just me locked in bone
sewn in the skin sack toting my ID

What I find on my porch is no mystery
I'm counting the folks I knew
born the century before last
      and checking my arithmetic
when Neighbor Jack Rabbit rolls up
      to the curb
with a sack of bean and beef burritos

a can of snoose and a six of Corona

Don't this look like a Friday night
         Jack says
and that sun and this town
         and that skyline
this or that or any America
Your grief's why him and who's next
You wonder why you this guy
         put his sins on plastic
when the bill's coming due

Hell we each travel a slippery road
across space and birthdays
to corruption in mud
         or burned to high heaven
Some say they know rightt for sure
When they drop and rot
         you'll see them
full of shit same as you

Jack's canted eyeball follows true
like a rat clattering down a drain

You out of luck and out of a job
and dead or dying's no joke
         but funny
you ain't yet eaten cat food
nor used cat for food
nor given up premium grass
Sure some question remains –
a year from now you might be
selling your ass on Main
         for a shot of Listerine

Sirens scream across brown lawns
and high as kites into the windy blue
Jack flicks a Newport butt into the street

We know we could be gone today
Why else you think we all so crazy
We beat our women and kids
and shoot anyone in the arc of our bullets
when what we need's the company
of a dog that stays off the bed

Maybe Westerns is where we go
            when we die
but no point hurrying
Come winter strike a light in the night —
            that's all a life's for
Rest easy
You're a poet with a pension
I'll dance on your grave for you
All you have to do is ask

Sundown on the Grampas
– August

My cows graze yellow grass
       down the slope
below these boot toes
scuffed in gray dirt
heels planted over a history
       dead as any Indian's –

buried busted sodbuster house
       sheds barn
and the yellow climbing rose
crucified on the yard fence
       each spring –

fingers rolling round and round
       a dark-chocolate shard
the heft enough to lift my feet
roll me through the hills
and down to the river

upstream and west to arrive
out of dust and gravel-stone ding

          *

Mom's at the dining room table
her fine blue ink loping
       across pages of a ledger
unsurprised
       had a feeling I'd show

We think *crockery*
We think *mixing bowl*
We talk ragged pioneer stories
patched with time's funny telling

how people dressed for town
        and church
Dad in a blue suit and hat
Mom in that brown tweed dress
my brothers' feet in polished shoes
this place and that place
the long dead folks who lived
        here and there

We *catch up*
We *visit*
We eat chicken and salad
        from cartons
The river flows beyond the cedars
        and apron of pale sand
just past the west window

*

The sun's patience makes summer
No toe-tapping
        checking the clock time
but long light
        early to late
by way of noon shadows
        shrunk to the soles of our feet

Soon the time of fat slow flies
Soon Orion back to hunt

winter days holes torn in the dark
night enough to talk over
       with the dead
why we're still standing

Summers' ghosts laugh that shit off
a rattle high in cottonwood leaves
       like fingers snapping
The answer's not virtue
and time only works if you let it

Tuckered
I lift my feet from the floor
fold myself fetal in a chair
       to chase down dreams
sure the sun'll be up soon
I fall asleep with my boots on
hand around sharp edges
       of a hard scrap

Frontier Dead as Romance

— September

Black as pitch at six when I rise for tea
Already too much of this year's sun
        pissed away

We collect red horses
in the ridge's long shadow
the day waits behind
coffee while they stand corralled
under Langenberg saddles
headstalls framing eyes
deep with all the dawns
the species has waited out

I'm learning to let be.

*

Above us a breeze spins
the windmill's galvanized blades
First light ricochets
off Fritz Elswick conchos
Sucker rod lifts and drops and lifts
Well water pulses out the spout
and it's time to climb
the northeast slope below the cedars
and gather cattle from fall grass
red and tall as my mare's eye
to cut three beeves
        down the alley

I invert my mug on a porch rail

*

Towards evening I lift a beer
to this sun now hot and blinding
against the porch's white wall
I declare life's post-debate coverage
        has signed off
Nothing I ain't done before
        under this sun
but trust morning's promise
        of early dark

Jump

– October

Riding a shadow in early dark
toward some future
null and void in this particular time

belaboring vision
like no tomorrow

a kind of personal reality therapy
date and day and my name
          on a whiteboard

pointless

while Dad in the '50s
drinks coffee from a Mason jar –

blue smoke from his Camel
the discarded pack I hold to my nose

the fresh plowed alfalfa ground
          we stand on

the B John Deere two-banger
          loud and belching exhaust

A Long Way from the Heart
– November

I'm sitting the fence again
      high heels hooked on a rail
      taller than the horses at my back
staring across the creek at grazed-down pasture
      drenched in unlikely sun

I believe in this bath of t-shirt weather
fear I'll fall with the catch of a spur
      or slip of a boot
and thinking on physics and anatomy
and stories of wrenched joints
      torn muscles
      cracked bones
guess these middle-aged horses
      the youngest I'll ride again

Later I'll climb aboard the midnight train
and when that westbound iron horse
      shudders into a lope
watch across the railyard
the city's color-coded parking garages
      drop away
before I crash for what sleep I'll get

to wake along the Eagle
      welcomed by sage and sandstone
        granite and pine
the election still a week away

and though I know the cold and snow
that fell to those natives

in loud-colored tents along the river
        two states north
will find me in a day or so
predictably sudden as concussion

my skin breathes only today's light
pictures of any tonight or tomorrow
no more real in the right now
than my neighbor's ripped flag this morning
       ragged stars and stripes
           twisting in the wind
      like me hanging by a thread

An Empty Country Owned by No One Here
– December

I got the dog baying across the alley
got whichever planet hangs in the west
and wouldn't ask Santa
for nothing I can get on my own

like this tobacco habit
that's got me out in the cold
walking streets to fix
this made-in-America curse

Who'd have thought some leaf
good only for pipe-circle talk
would have me skating thin ice
flailing in a gale like an unrigged sail
this night of the day the Corps did justice

I guess some grandfather people
like these young veterans
and all who stand
under this dry winter child
our moon growing in a clear sky
to remind each alone and windblown
       one of us

with its out-of-season jack-o-lantern grin
of the scowls pocking Facebook
and the president-elect's default grimace

You try trusting a man who don't laugh

Out of a job my ambition's natural
this close to the holidays
        and Wounded Knee –
a future that'll survive me

protectors along all fingers
        of the Big River
a place of ruminants and wolves
some switchgrass ethanol
a people light on their feet
        and dug in for the long haul

No more no-till mudslides
collateral damage of chemical runoff
or downstream flood of the last of my tribe
to hunt and gather lives from these plains

No medivac frostbite cases
Just for once no victims
only a new moon's smile

hopeful as the retro graphic
        on my wall calendar
among columns of days
and dates we march through
toward a red Christmas

Coda

Multiverse

Nowadays I hear my name in traffic
        walk up to strangers'
                wooden-toothed smiles
                        their laminated cheeks
my right hand fisted

No thing now –
        with constant coverage
                of killer cops
                        and walking women –
to move in time

I'm the boy in winter sneaking a peek
in an upstairs trunk
        at Dad's woolen uniform
                chevron and six hash marks
                        on the sleeve
I fear Fascists in the bottom of my soft belly

I'm the boy in summer in a dark pasture
        searching the speckled
                and belted sky
                        for Sputnik
Russians scare me to a sweat

Today's dimension of fogbound space's
        tougher to leave behind
                my walk around the hood
                        a spade I'll use to dig out
the town I know exists

Shadows in swirling pearl —
  a tree
    a tree
      a man
standing in the bed of a pickup

When I speak he jumps as if I'd broken out
   of the goose mist
     in feathers and breechclout
I smell blood on the coming rain

Dinah, Won't You Blow Your Horn

Stations of the Cross

Tonight I'm a cartoon drunk
      in an alley
on my way home from a bar
circling my dropped hat
for the correct geometry
each hiccup a puff of breeze
fluffing my winter hair

Walking women on the street
caught in the corner of my eye
call a spade a spade
That man a guilty boy
I'm in no shape to argue
My sins run stride for stride
with outlaws and outsiders
across years and pages
      and imagined skies

Each hand of cards tells two tales –
better to die a part of
      if alone
and winter's an ornery fact
Soon I'll be flat on my back
      as a prairie skyline
my mind an open plain

just one more in a row of cowboys
leaning on a bar in a Bassett saloon
heading to a dance next month
in a town called Rose

Boys I'll say *take it*
> *from a big-bellied silverback*
and remember
he said
> *she said*
Baby I'd go with you to Mullen
> *but all our shit's in Valentine*

For the Duration

1

All the summer I've wasted
month after month stitched
      nose to tail
along some high sunny slope
      with just enough work
         to make it work
and when the work was through
the day done and the sun down
a barn full of iced beer

And to end up again right here
in soft clothes in a warm house
      snow on the roof
at my elbow a dark picture window
      against the west wind
my lenses mirrored in a screen
on one in a long line of longest nights
dropping like a domino in winter syrup

And to what end
      but to judge
the now and then
in currency of hair and belly
cattle and horse
cowboy morphed to password

2

Still I've keys at my fingertips
to unlock the blank screen
      of my brain

some little invention left
in my sad story-telling soul
an imaginary friend to croon
        me a bedtime story
about a fella we both know
He'll step up to the mic
        like he's brave

3

Forty years on the job
wear a uniform each
        and every day
my own peculiar Halloween
I've seen a lot —
fubar following snafu
in a regular clockwork clusterfuck

I rise each morning
        with the factory whistle
launch across Central Standard Time
aboard a town named for some
        railroad baron's niece

Christmas
        I get Jack on the horn
to check his politics
on what the government says —
adults smoking grass
doubled in the last ten years

Line dead like his mind
        gone on that stuff
and then all Jack says
        he's pretty sure

he don't smoke twice as much

Rats in the henhouse
            man
You understand that's all
            he understood
I tell you he's a fine-fingered fella
been raking the ashes of a cold fire
            too long

            4

The dream tells the story
or is it our waking minds
that assemble the dismembered
            fragments
plays Doctor Frankenstein
manhandling dead flesh
suturing beginning middle and end

            5

Down to the lumber yard
some mother screams
her child in danger

Three bass beats
He wakes behind the wheel
snake eyes popping up fresh

He turns the key

            6

Go to the weather

always works for me

The windshield cinema
        along the highway
bones of corn under snow
Out beyond gravel
spotted cattle half hid in red grass
        and scrub cedars

What I've read and believe
before roads
        bison on bald hills
not the dream of a tree in sight

What is and what was
        time in my pocket
Who wakes who sleeps
        the sum of what will be

7

Just to fall asleep to the screech
of an angry lady teacher next door
her lesson plan a benediction
        I earned –

I can't seem to make it work
White mice'll be by later today
        to fix the tech
For next time cut to the hard work
        of manners and discussion
Meanwhile talk talk talk
        amongst yourselves

        – for John

Bound Away

"not one splotched
   rightside-up sundown
   paint-by-numbers skyline"
      — Jack Brown

I'm out tonight drinking tap Pabst
lukewarm as summer baths
listening to a good beer-garden band
in my boogie shoes —
Wyoming snakebite boots
         near to my knees
tall heels good for teetering —
the band and crowd and me
a living thing in a downtown
so dead that earlier one buzzard
among the oblivious scores roosting
         atop the city cell tower
hanged himself and still undead
         dangled
by a foot coiled in coaxial cable
and swung in slow wing-flaps
         of embarrassed resignation

But for the blood running
         to my head
maybe not a bad way to go
loose cannon hanging by a thread
after a past upended on cedar posts
like worn Texas slippers
         and weighty Sheridan mules
dotting the fenceline behind me
earth and heaven my only frame

Here and now across the wide Missouri
rock and roll banks off the red-brick
backside of a century-and-a-quarter old
　　　main-street storefront
some Victorian merchant's frontier vision
from a time of young dreamers
now buried deep and long ago
all futures sidewinders hiding
　　　in tall grass

Los Caballos

I cut the cord
unleash the dog of cable
to roam and fatten on others

a poor front-porch joke
no ones hears
among the siren songs
rolling south down Logan
like pinball paying off
out to the dark highway
toward horse country

where no one much
knows his sire
nor cares to
like we city folk must

Lightning marches this way
Tomorrow will tell –
summer-night velocity
young men in wreckage
fuel and flames

Days and nights
Sons and fathers
like the guy in a suitcoat
a career demands
and a flu-ridden kid
pale as the waning moon

Or the drunk clawing
his old man's second-hand

furniture into a nest
of constituent chips and rags

Yes it can be better
Of course it could be worse –

Not a prayer with a papa
who won't love you
enough to let you
be and believe
in other gods
or none at all

And then – surprise!
we fathers just die
bequeathing the debts
and cares that wore
us onionskin thin

No simple plug to pull
nor coaxial to disconnect
sons carry the evil
and good of us lifetimes
We die hard

This storm's missed me –
lightning past
klaxons quiet
while someone's son lies
like jangled cutlery
on a high table

Luck of the draw
Tomorrow I'll tote

my dad – that long-gone
profane holy man –
up out of these
humid heartbreak flats
into the thin air
of our continent's spine
to stand bewildered
by the long view

White Buffalo

Ain't hardly no one left out here
        on these Anglo Plains
each white man surrendering
to dreams bigger than his own

like Gibbie come up all this way
to show northern hands
        how to cowboy
just now this Christmas
        boarding this bus
for Back Home Oklahoma
on a ticket I bought him
        like Saint Nick
his outfit stuffed in two pillowcases

like the end of the story
that starts with Mom's folks
        on the platform
amid locomotive coal smoke
in long coats and dresses
carpetbags dragging white knuckles
the old tongue lolling in their heads

where some breed cowboy
        up out of the Nations
lounging against the depot wall
        drawled directions
and pointed through
        the dust of the street
out onto the treeless rises
his handrolled's red coal
the steel tip of a plowshare

Kicking Up Iron

"What's this one about?"
      – EJMB

Damned if I know anything
beyond what's right under my nose
      and plain before my eyes

just enough corral to hold a few
      gentled horses –

poles peeling bark
      white as Halloween bones

and a rickety windmill tower
from one spent century or the other

What's the difference
My point exactly

1880 or 1910
it still pumps water
      from the same shallow well

through long cobbled-together pipe
      over and at right angles
to the current of a cattail-choked creek

into a fiberglass fish hatchery tank
      circa 1960
to water the simple thirst of big cattle

Water flowing east
Water flowing north

and from above

After each rain mud at my feet
yields another crop of scrap

I collect in a Storz beer cooler
          of 1950s aluminum
                    on the bunkhouse porch –

pitted and pocked nuts and bolts
          spikes
                    square-headed nails

sometimes heavy cast parts and pieces
          no one I know can name

Such was the world made for me
Such is the world I've wrought –

a head full of bright orange rust
and half-buried toe-stubbing chunks
          of guilt

steel I trip over in the dark of my mind
after each freshet and cloudburst –

the stories I take to my grave
my practice not to tell any tale
          straight

but to follow the first tangent
          I come to –

a finger along lines in my scalp
          tracing maps of old scars

When All Blood Is Shadow

    por Ezechiel

Winter nights of clear weather
I drive state highways late
        after traffic's gone –
white moon
      gray earth
           black shadow

Funny sort of thing to think
on a hot dry summer afternoon
      of elemental colors –
high blue sky
      green grass
          red blood

across the back of my hand
from the RedBrand wire
of the new fence we're stringing –
four glinting strands
      black creosote
          posts of green steel

Not the blood of murdered bison
nor the people who made meat
      for winter
no matter how sweet
      and cheap
          that lie would be

just aspirin-thinned blood
from a shallow cut

of a red-painted barb
across the parchment skin
of an old white man

I bleed for me
My cows graze
where bison roamed
I fence out neighbors' corn
and neighbors' machines
and poisons
all
their ready-for-the-Roundup
soybeans

Just another customer for salvation
I fence for my personal Jesus –
runty neighbor
one-eyed Merle Jacobsen
who didn't survive
eighth grade

Who better
What better
Late night blizzard
wind in the wire
Among cedars
cows big as buffalo
nostrils fringed with frost
hearts pumping hot

The Life

Quit cows
Quit the ponies
Quit beer
Quit the whiskey
       and wine

Stay off the grass

Quit night in summer
Quit day in winter.
Quit the streak
Go cold turkey

Get it right
Write it down
Say good night
Say good day

LA Suite

Uber Driver and the Armenian Dream

Seven hundred
twenty thousand miles
over the road
Nebraska Wyoming sure
mile marker ten thirty-three
popcorn on left
popcorn on right

In America things straight
In Ukraine you drunk
drive hundred miles an hour
your brother policeman
no problem
Here everybody go to jail

Wife here longer
better English
These houses
two-bedroom two-bath
Million dollars

Where we live
three boys
go to school
come home
stay inside
go to sleep
get up
go to school
In Los Angeles
everybody confused

Red Bluff
mile marker 550
house cheap
Big sale one day each week
Everybody buy and sell
Wife nine months finish
medical-billing school
We go there
raise sheep
like in Ukraine

At the Foot of Hank's Grave

When we ask
old woman smiles
shakes her head
tells us
I'm Chinese.

Trumpet-playing grandson
pitch perfect English
his smile twin to hers
not a note of help

Busted experiments fail
only if we refute the lesson –
better to be lucky than good

Bourbon poured
out of a plastic skin
Ocean View Cemetery
no ocean view
but the skeletal top
reaches of the derricks
of the port of LA

Sobering experience
bareheaded
to recall a beginning
in this breath
and count clean to the bone
on a surefire end

My sort of pride
a last imagined virtue
just any sack of bones
authoring a travelogue
as a labor of love
And the joke's on me
when I stand
to brush grave dirt
off my black brim
Fading stars
planted in these hills
laugh at
not with me

Vision

The red in blood
an iron compass needle
points to prehistory

This Chumash on a flat rock
alone among
orange petals of poppies

fluttering in the breeze
mirrored in clean river water
salt surf crashing in the west

His eyes set with the sun
and rise to street-lit night
under the overpass

the nylon of his tent
smudged the color
of a filthy rind

Boxed Chablis at his hip
one drinking man
in a city of tents

of traffic hum
and stars of window lights
climbing to the moon

He howls
a mushroom of lightning
under his lids

after Bonnie Johnson-Bartee and for Chad Christensen

Someone's in the Kitchen

Howdy

How you all doing this cold winter night
I drove down the last of the light
thinking I'd run out of map
when I seen your neon
      flickering like twisting snakes
The way you write your name
      in the sky's all the invite
I need

I taps the pedal and says to myself
      Get off this goddamned road
step out for a breath of January air
though cold as hell if hell was cold

Like the eyes of this mean girl
one time at a party on the stairs
      above me
I seen the snake tongue of an idea
      flicker cross her black irises
She don't hesitate long enough
for me to click my heels
      and wish for Kansas
She did more than scratch my pride –
had to go sit down for an hour
You know you remember
the hardest you been kicked there
Hindsight's knowing never approach
a mystery with too wide a stance
I been taught by my betters again
      and again

You got a Diet Coke in a can

I'd rather warm
      if they all ain't in the cooler
and I'll pass on ice on a night such as this

I guess I'm that proverbial stranger
      folks talk about
who drifts into town though
      all I've seen hereabouts
so far is just this crossroads bar
Getting lost's just a matter
      of following my nose
One thing you learn on the road
coming and going don't do nothing
      but chase each other around

Same with what that mean girl taught me
One hot summer –
      furthest thing from the hungry bear
            clawing on the door tonight –
big doughboy dogging me
      at some backyard party
arguing same old shit I was long
      worn out on
and I guess I opened my mouth
      like I'm known to do
when I might have kept it closed
but instead said just the perfect
      wrong thing
I seen the blur
      of his big bucket fist
            coming at the end
                  of a wide roundhouse

I was still standing when the little birdies
      flew away singing

I seen he dropped into his crouch
dukes up like he was acting the part
feet spread like he's straddling
          the Dakotas
Couldn't ask for a better gunsight
He dropped like timber
All that fat jiggled once
and settled in like landscape
When I leaned down to get in the last word
he had the same dumb look dying animals get

I'd write that girl a thank-you note
          on pretty paper
for drawing me a map
          if I knew
which pen she ended up in

Would you grab me some of them
          sour cream and onion potato chips
Please and thank you
Just like Mother used to make

☙

Part of the art of road's knowing

a friendly face or three's
          good as an oak chunk fire
in Grandma's nickel-plated parlor stove

You all from around here

Sorry I pontificate
like this fella with the big nose
my old man took me in a tavern

I suppose to see about a horse
one egg-and-daughter night back home
tooting his own horn
about his new green '57 Pontiac

Maybe four or five
        I couldn't've been more than knee-high
Dad and the man with the horse
drank Storz draws from pilsner glasses
and me I sucked on an orange Nehi
till the sugar ran out my ears
I recall the butane smell of World War Zippos
a carnival of scattered nickels and dimes
around a bright pack of Luckies
        on a scarred mahogany bar
and glittering up over my head
a land-of-sky-blue-waters sign

Pretty soon I had to pee fast
like only little kids and old men do
You all remember your first men's room
All cigarette butts and one of them pink cakes
        drownt in yellow piss
The joints I land in mostly ain't changed much
This place here looks to be a step up for me

First bar stool I ever climbed up
        and down off of
Ain't met one yet I can't ride
though I damn near been throwed
        a time or two
I credit my luck to good friends
        and a lifetime of training
Used to drink most the night
        like it's my day job

but I give up the beer and the whiskey
        for the sake of sobriety
got my collection of chips for testimony
but still enjoy a good gab

I've got the one other habit
I doubt I'll shake till it cashes me in
Any other weather I'd just step out
If no one's bound to enforce the law
        for the next five minutes
I'd be grateful for an empty to tap ash in

Mostly I tell folks the truth
        as they should see it
I don't need to be liked
but since crying's too common
I'll appeal to their sense of humor
        if they got one
Funny how folks don't laugh though
when they hear how and where Elvis died
Like that fella told me one time
All pure products of America go crazy
Think about it you see he's right

I remember old Ed Sullivan
        on the black and white
I witnessed the King crazy-legging
through a fuzzy rural coat-hanger antenna
America ain't never seen nothing like that
        before
I'm special that night
sitting right between the folks on the old davenport
while the rest of the litter's scattered across the floor
Pops into my head to say –
way I'm put together

if something's shows up there
            it comes out here –
He looks to need to go to the bathroom
First laugh I got that I recall

Different time back then
We didn't say pee or piss
much less all them worse words
Now they say all that shit on TV
And our bathroom was a tin tub
on the kitchen floor Saturday nights
For the other we had a little house out back
or real cold nights like this one here
a five-gallon bucket in the kitchen
            half full of dirty dishwater
Bathroom's what we said to be polite
Back then the folks wanted something
            better for us than tenant-farming
which ain't nothing but share-cropping
            come north

If the supply of Diet Coke ain't run dry
            I'll take another

⌒

It's all modern now

            like that's supposed to be better
but I don't know
Half the people I grew up with already dead
Each had a song and a story to tell
though only here and there
            did anyone listen
and few of us heard a thing right

The rest moved to Colorado
or California for jobs and weather
Don't blame 'em on a day like this
Dry cold like hell's a dry heat
like that's supposed to be better too

Hell ain't nobody left but me
       and you all
ma'am
       and gentlemen

I can see by your outfits
you all cowboyed some
Stands to reason being
where you be in this state of grass
You all know the trick to stock
Except for a pet cow or two
we're all just passing through

I've cowed all my life
       one way or the other
Folks had me out back in the barn
black morning and night
feeding milk from a dozen shorthorn
       crossbreds to bucket calves
after the cream been skimmed

When I was eight or ten
they give me a one-legged stool
       all my own
and put me on a couple Brown Swiss –
       Molly and Sally
You know how it goes –

stick your cap in a flank
a bucket between your knees
go to pulling tits
and ducking shit-flinging tails
No breakfast nor supper
till after the pigs been slopped
            eggs gathered
and them cows milked
stripped and turned out
            twice a day
and cold church Sundays

Course I know they don't do it
            that way no more
and that's alright by me
cause I ain't going back
no matter what milking machine
patent some smart guy files

The winter my babiest brother's born
like this one
            maybe a little worse
                  probably not
Bad enough
            Mama boarded at her grandma's
                  and maiden aunt's
in the nearest town with a hospital
The day they called Dad
            to make his way there
                  through them winter hills
left my oldest brother
            me and the sister between us
to milk the cows that night

Cold and dark and chores taking forever
            and some big redbone
even hobbled bout doubled-hocked
            my sister to the moon
My oldest brother's the boss and all
            and while he's yelling at her
            and while she's shivering and crying
                snot running out her nose
I was thinking *plenty of gentle cows left*
But he ain't happy till he completes
            the gesture
and sends her to the house
            to watch the little boys

So now we're down to just us two
We milk and milk and milk and milk
sticking our hands up under the flank
to keep our bare frozen fingers
            from falling off
When we're down to stripping
            our last cows
Dad comes rolling in
            grin big as a door
his town clothes still fresh
            announces *It's a boy*
like he's hammering a bell
and I thought *Good*
            he can milk these bossies

And that's what he does to this day
            last I checked
and him a man only ten years younger
            than me

I skinned out soon as I was able
took up ranch work as more suitable
for a fella of my refined sensibility
Besides folks had all the boys they needed
   to feed

        ⅎ

You see as a kid I composed a life

   of dog-eared pages
flickering movie screens
   and TV heroes
meting out justice in the snow
   of poor reception

I reckon
   I ain't telling you nothing
you don't know
when I say it ain't like in the movies
nor them Charlie Russell Montana paintings
forking a silver-studded saddle
running with a longhorn stampede
   amidst the lightning strikes
More buck rakes and beaverslide stackers
cedar posts and rusty barbwire
crooked steeples and bent nails
three-tined pitchforks and moldy alfalfa

Mostly I like the calving
   though I can't exactly say why
when any birth's an iffy proposition
Prolapses in the mud
   dismemberments

and c-sections
an X from ears to eyes
           and a short gun's bark
Some mama cow who'll end up
feedlot beef for some dentist's cook-out
holding a three-day wake over her dead calf
Some unfortunate little critter drowned
           in amniotic fluid
tongue swollen and out
cold and stiff to the touch
eyes that only glimpsed the light –

Well hell that ain't the liking part
Just cold days make for cold tales

But what I've seen gives me faith in cows
I've sat above a half dozen
like so many midwives
like spokes in a wagon wheel
nosing a down heifer in her first calving
They know better than any cowboy can
And on a sunny day
week-old calves hightailing across the range
bucking and circling and playing
           their baby bovine games
cools any ambitions I get to make a change

None and all of it sums up
to a non-arithmetical balance
Tell the truth for all the horror
my bull-sized fear's when one spring
I won't be around for it any more
I think about that every meal
           when I eat my meat

I'll be damned
You boys look froze as my bones

Miss what's your handle anyway

⚭

Verlene

That's catchy as a pop tune
Here's five dollars for the juke
and get these boys what they're drinking
      out of this other
Keep it soft so we don't got to shout
Just a nice shake and rattle back behind
      these stories I'm telling
Just don't want to resort to yelling

They won't say it from no Nevada stage
and I ain't one of them buckaroos
they write spur-jingle pomes about
all hat and boots and bullshit
hawking and spitting classic cowboy songs

You take your cowboy poets –
      least most of them –
any old man at the bar's sad and solemn
broke but full of worldly experience
      with the accent on the *ex*
and no future *perience* on the skyline

Any woman's just too good for mortal man
each is the best horse ever sprouted hair

and even the dogs mostly behave
  decent obedient and brave
while the West's closing down
  from too much government
which is where all the hippies went
  to work
after they ruint the country

I ain't fond of many of them professors
  neither
where the fine point of a short po*em's*
whether its tipend's enough
  to earn an academic stipend
Me I dwell closer to home
Hell you tell me if any of life's scribblings
  are worth your time
with or without the rhyme

You all know though much as I whine
cows ain't really *the* purpose at all
Give me a horse –
not one with too much gas
  or I'm ass
over teakettle –
pardon my French Verlene
I'll hit the happy trail
in my good roping saddle
  at the drop of any hat

I can't count the times that cantle
come up to spank my backside
I always feared I couldn't stick a horse
and to be honest sometimes I didn't
I suppose that's why I've ridden

the same
four-year-old brown nag
        for twenty years now
My age you don't put on airs
I keep away from cranky mares

Still I always like to think
one more good horse waits yet
out there ahead of me
before I reach the final pasture gate
like I always wished I could sing
        and pick a guitar riding through
But one hand on the strings
trying to locate that lurking music
leaves me singing monotonal
        and anecdotal
while the second hand might as well
        scratch scrotal
for all the tune it makes

                              ∽

Verlene I will have another

Anyway spring summer and fall
cows and horses be my living
Make of that what you will

I don't cotton to winter chores
        no more
I seen too many of them
        blue-cloud fronts ride in
I done my time amidst the drifts
        of a hundred big storms

when white wind peppers the sky
whips the world to a froth of shapes
remakes creation to kingdom come

And then always after the snow
        the deep cold --
not always like tonight but cold –
air like lead in the lungs
ground froze hard as Earth's first rock
feet I fret to feel again
        for the pins and needles

And when we get a little thaw
and I hit whichever bar to celebrate
I end up sick from whatever bug's
        going around
Headache pulsing to my heartbeat
Sinuses packed and mouth-breathing
Lungs like greasy paper sacks
Dizzy all the time
and no cure like the old farmer
        with his feet in a basin
sucking on a jug of blackberry brandy
I got no wife handy
        to keep adding
hot water from the steam kettle

Oh I surely do like women
kept company with one or another
        different times
Only baby sitter folks ever got us kids –
I was probably three or four –
put me up in her lap to teach me
        to French kiss

which'll encourage an early interest
        in grown-up matters
If she walked in right now
I believe I'd drop to one knee
and propose to Brenda Brown
        old as she must be

I can get teary-eyed sentimental
and tread on the edge of a canyon
        of regret
recollecting this time or that —
dance halls and early morning rides
        in the rising sun
buck-naked river swims and bubble baths
the Christmas blizzard of aught-nine
drinking red wine in two upstairs rooms
        I rented in town
from the local parish that winter
Hell I could have died married
        and a Baptist
if I'd've just crossed the street
        of a Sunday morning

but I could never shake the notion
that a codependent life's a slow death
        with what's eating you

Besides
        hard to keep a woman with you
when all you offer's Saturday nights
Down's wherever gravity pulls you

࿆

Winters now I drift

      an read
a drifting of its own
me like a baby in my bed
rocking to the rhythm of a voice
I invite inside my head
Company I guess

But voices sum up in weeks and months
of short dark days inside four walls
        to cabin fever
Pretty soon I'm winking back
        at my prick
like he's a one-eyed cattle buyer
          spending other folks' money
on cows he don't want to own
        and thinking
all that low-hanging fruit's got a point

I like to take a month or so to go it alone
get to the top of the mountain
        for the long view
so to say
        in particular
if I can find a woman to help
Any cold's difficult to paddle right
         speaking metaphoric
for a little lost man adrift in a boat
I don't mean to be cryptic
I just can't let the tease of hope
        lay fallow

My habit's to hang tight past January

When icicles begin to drip from the eaves
I trade books back in for hooks
      and climb aboard
for one good rock and roll country holler
with a cowboy promise to follow
that note up any sky-bound yodel

We're just talking here
I can't say what you all see
through the hoarfrost
on these windows over your shoulders
      hermanos
For me that streetlamp shines a spider web
I see cold jewels like Ferris wheel lights

But this winter I jumped some early
      against doctor's orders as it were
drifted out of them Paradise Hills before my time
The truth's I went looking for a thaw out of season
      though I defy any soothsayer to say
how I got turned around
      and gone wrong this far

Like the city cousin said
when he left the outhouse
What'll they think of next

∽

Something's been off from the start

I been a man finding his way
      in a dark house he don't know
I been edgy and itchy

with the need to confess
a crime I can't find a name for
I'd had my bull parts checked
        like you do in any herd
Maybe it was just the usual suspense
like waiting for the news
        after peeing on a stick

Anyway call came saying this new hat –
        silverbelly and smooth as water –
I ordered custom-built with my fall wages
        waited ready down in the city
I didn't even think for a minute to hesitate
        but loaded up my warbag
with the leftovers of the usual necessities
        and on the way out
paid a call on Utah Charley –
        a thinking man and good a friend
                as I got left –
up at his lineshack in that lonely country
hoping he'd help me get my affairs in order

Sort of surprised when he meets me
        at the door
said *Thought a green horse'd got you*
        by now

He's paper-patching a roll-your-own
        with spit
He's *deef* but catches my gist
and talks like he ain't out of practice

Doctors tell you what's wrong
but not so much what's right

Who rides into town
        shoots the villain and travels on
Movie heroes mostly survive
        against all odds
Not so much in books
        and less in life

I'm riding the step in the doorway
        between his two rooms
his tight-strung banjo hung from pegs
        by my ear
so every word he says rung in my head
        true or not

In a life of error
I made only one fatal mistake
        so far
and that long ago
And it really weren't my fault
He only looked up to me
        and once or twice took my advice
back when I's too ignorant not to give it

His girlfriend didn't cheat on him
        with me
I ain't the father of her twins
        nothing like that
but ever notice how contagious
        heartbreak can be

I kept this picture of myself
every morning the mirror proved untrue
I see now the fairy tales don't lie
We're all food for some ogre

What's beneath the bridge
*   eats us all*

Ah hell you can't have a road
that don't run two ways
but to ride his black horse down
*   to hell*
a toe in a .30-30's trigger guard —
it's made mine a grumpy life

I don't know why it had to be
*   that or any way*
Rock and roll hard as you can
Nobody's happy when the party ends

Verlene – the look of loss about you
            like your good red dog died
and you hombres all quiet
            like you playing statuary

I'd like to know what you savvy
of this caballero del norte

Keep it to yourselves then I guess
            mis amigos
Ain't my place to pry

I was young for a long time
            but oh these bones
                    this overblown flesh –
what moves bruises
An old man has to think to stand
            before he rises
and a thought's like a cranky motor

grinding
        trying to catch

I should grit my teeth and quit
      I suppose
but I'll tell the rest if I can keep
      the pieces
from sliding like Texans on ice
If confession's good for the soul
      I'll keep on talking
till I've told it all and then some
though I expect time's past gone for it
I had just the one more stop to make
      on my way

ॐ

Ma

I says
      when I walk through the door
your wandering boy's returned
She's got her rocker under a reading lamp
      her cane hooked on the arm
a Bible on the stand beside her
and an open book bout politics on her lap

Her daddy raised her Democrat
and these days she worries a lot
      about of the other side
A bone-deep Christian lady who knows
      her Gospels
she don't pass judgement on any glass house
Still she thinks they oughtn't make up

what Jesus says or what Jesus'd do
like putting kids in cages
at least until they've come of age

Maybe you got kids Verlene
        maybe not
No offense intended either way
but ain't nothing like having a mother
        to make me feel guilty
like her just sitting there sweeter than anyone
        has a right to be
brighter and sharper than a ten-penny nail
reminds me without a word
        just by being
of all she did to bring me
        into this world and raise me up
and how little but live I've done with it

She's seen a century and still
keeps her own house near the river
        frozen over this winter
I watched out the window past her shoulder
while a lot of folks younger than her
have to check the white board at the home
        just to know it's Tuesday
No one's left who's known her all her life —
        maybe a curse but she don't act it
Some ancient thing not exactly herself
        resides within her
shines out from deep inside
        like an angel Buddha or sea stone

She kept the brood of us fed and schooled
        and alive

when something was always dying –
a spotted horse
        a Durham milk cow
            laying hens
milk barn cats
       an old cowdog
or the Pawnee neighbor from over the hill
       in his shack on the dry creek bed –
until now we're upright standing adults
       scattered but with good marriages
           and their own grandchildren
Except for me
      Miserable sinner that I am
         she never mentions my failings
constant as they are

Even knowing better I slept sound that night
      for the first time this winter
dreaming of sculpted madonnas
      and icy baptisms and peace
and knowing all rivers are the same water
and what home I've got's under my mama's roof
We breakfasted early
      I hayed the two pensioner cows she keeps
        like museum pieces
and pointed the pickup downriver to the city
      for to fit my new hat

☙

What's a cow know

     of straight lines and Sundays
I expect I look a fright

All I wanted
            was my new water-smooth silverbelly
but this fresh Montana crease in the crown's
            already stomped out
Here I sit split-knuckled in freeze-dried blood
            and my cowboy drag
like an old car-wrecked rodeo queen
            been through the windshield
behind me a childhood of machine-mangled
and war-wounded one-armed men
and winter women wearing pants
            under their dresses

Should've taken a Saturday night bath
but my dream was to see people again
            blow off some winter steam
in the city where all rivers meet –
mail carriers on their march-of-the-penguins
            delivery
busy-street exhaust like warm pools
            I should dive into

For a place to stay I like a little fancy –
I was probably the only one standing
at the big hotel wearing winter drawers
I'd overheard enough from the crowd
            in the hotel lounge –
young people thick as flyspecks
            on an August outhouse
                  Sears & Roebuck catalogue –
and I was tired of trying to decipher the Greek
            of performative authentic selves
from twenty-somethings woke
            as Hollywood tan lines

My standard in saloons runs more
        the other way
and my nose for dives makes for a short hunt
Just the dry drunk at the near end of the bar
        I was talking to strangers like now
telling the joke about the lady
        named her poodle Ballsitch –
which was funnier back when
        folks carried pocket change –
and waiting on this little band to take
        the stage for another set

Music's about all that'll stop my talk
I seen sparks from this fella's jangling guitar
and that bassline and them voodoo drums
        punched at my heart –
like I say when it comes to music
        bout all I can attempt's
           to keep the beat –
when some sneaking tweaker
        hurrying by with a fresh beer
like he's heading to his regular pew
up in sniffers' row at an Oklahoma oil wrestling
passed behind my stool
        brushed my brim
           knocked my brand new hat
cockeyed

Made me mad
        enough to call his mother a name
which maybe I oughtn't have done
 My reflexes ain't what they was
        but I got my licks in

before a cyclone bomb I didn't see coming
divorced me from my conscious mind
I must've dropped like a sack of Portland

I come to in a puddle of whiskey
        and beer and broken glass
Blood speckled on bystanders' winter boots
        and pooling on the floor

Guess I just left –
I never dallied no time hanging
round the kind of trouble
        that'll draw John Law
Tell the truth I don't recall
        getting up at all
but here I am with you

I know I drove all night
that old pickup just motoring on
something wrong with the fuel gauge
red sunup flaming in the rearview
behind clouds like black smoke
all day in this blood and frost
on a highway empty of traffic
past lost farms
        swallowed in scrub elms
through dead-eyed towns
        not a soul in sight

                ∞

Must be hell

You all laugh like fresh meat

at an AA meeting
like I owe you money
like you got to smell a joke
before you make a human face
I believe I'll smoke another
maybe warm up the tip
of my broken nose
I used to think the truth's not what you say
so much as how you say it
I suppose living and believing like I done
gave that fella every right
to send me down
I see I've followed my final footsteps
to this place
At last I know how it goes

Cutty on rocks for me Verlene
a double
and an another round for this house
of godforsaken broken-hearted sinners
Look for Robert Johnson on the juke

Something suitable for shaking hands
with the devil

I know you know right now
what I'd trade for one more season
but the view from this barstool's
getting foreshortened
At this angle I'm a little man
grown smaller
some fool to think I'd ever leave
this winter behind

I see now everyone
   and everything's beautiful –
from the overlord of the underworld
   to ice –
if you find the spot to catch the light
   just right

Notes

The two standard methods of roping stock from horseback are mentioned in "Derby Day." "Tied hard and fast" is what it says – the tail of the rope knotted around the horn – and has the advantage of keeping a critter, once roped, securely caught. The primary disadvantage is that it leaves the roper without recourse in case of a wreck. "Dallies" (from Spanish, like much cowboy lingo) are the turns of the tail of the rope around the horn ropers make after the critter is caught. The technique is especially important when roping larger animals.

A "correction line," as mentioned in "Right Side of History" is one of an occasional short east-west jogs in a grid of section roads that accommodate the narrowing of the earth in higher latitudes. The "Kinkaid Act" (1904), named for its sponsor, Nebraska Congressman Moses P. Kinkaid, amended the Homestead Act, granting patents for larger tracts of land (640 acres, a section) in areas less suited to conventional agriculture.

"A Long Way from the Heart" makes oblique reference to the protest, led by the Standing Rock Sioux, against the proposed Keystone XL pipeline

The partial line "the day the Corps did justice" in "An Empty Country Owned by No One Here" refers to the Army Corps of Engineers' denial of an easement for the building of the Keystone XL pipeline under the Missouri River. It proved only a temporary victory.

"*All pure products of American go crazy,*" from the "Verlene I'll have another" section of "Someone's in the Kitchen" is a slight corruption of the opening two lines of William Carlos Williams' "For Elsie."

Acknowledgments

My gratitude to the editors of these journals for publishing the following poems:

Clover, "An Empty Country Owned by No One Here," "Frontier Dead as Romance" and "The Poor Mouth Talking Cure;"; *Concho River Review,* "Kicking Up Iron" and "A Long Way from the Heart;"; *San Pedro River Review,* "Bound Away," "Stations of the Cross" and "Derby Day."

And my thanks to Tana Buoy, Neil Harrison, Bonnie Johnson-Bartee, Maureen Kingston and Grizz McIntosh who saw these poems in their early drafts. Their reactions and suggestions were a great help to me.

Finally, I want to thank David Lee for his sage advice on "Someone's in the Kitchen."

I've been working on the railroad
All the live-long day.
I've been working on the railroad
Just to pass the time away.
Can't you hear the whistle blowing,
Rise up so early in the morn;
Can't you hear the captain shouting,
"Dinah, blow your horn!"

Dinah, won't you blow,
Dinah, won't you blow,
Dinah, won't you blow your horn?
Dinah, won't you blow,
Dinah, won't you blow,
Dinah, won't you blow your horn?

Someone's in the kitchen with Dinah
Someone's in the kitchen I know
Someone's in the kitchen with Dinah
Strummin' on the old banjo!

Singin' fee, fie, fiddly-i-o
Fee, fie, fiddly-i-o-o-o-o
Fee, fie, fiddly-i-o
Strummin' on the old banjo.

CPSIA information can be obtained
at www.ICGtesting.com
Printed in the USA
LVHW111545120822
725815LV00005B/538